25%

Suthida Chang

Presentation by *BookLeaf Publishing*

Web: www.bookleafpub.com

E-mail: info@bookleafpub.com

ISBN: 978-93-5744-442-2

First edition 2022

DEDICATION

To myself, the people I know and don't know, and to every stranger I've crossed paths with in the past, present and future.

Me

Soft purples and periwinkles are a delight.
Unwritten writings stored in sight.
Thoughtful and a bit dreamy at times.
History and philosophy interest her mind.
Invigorated by feasts and fantasies.
Daring to question what doesn't seem right.
Alas, we met.

Live

Tik, tok,
The clock's racing.
Not waiting for you,
Who's lost and misplaced.

Knock, knock,
You have a visitor!Is it time for new adventures?
Or is it delivery for your dentures?

Thud, thud,
Are those footsteps approaching the door?
Or is it your aspirations
Crashing into the floor?

Swish, swish,
It's a shooting star!
Are you still not chasing
A life worth living?

Mornings

We'd wake up to the sound of chattering,
Laughing and the occasional bickering.
Of rubber soles crushing sand and stone,
And pots and pans clinking against the stove.

Mama opens our window to let in the crisp air,
"Get out of bed!" She'll joyfully declare.
With sleepy eyes we'd follow the smell of food
That always puts us in a pleasant mood.

Our mornings are filled with familiar faces,
Shaven, bearded, furry, and whiskered.
Gathered around a chiseled wood table,
Missing an inch so slightly unstable.

After the eating comes the cleaning,
And mopping, brushing and more sweeping.
Under the coconut trees, we'd rest a bit,
Then onwards with new journeys, we commit.

C-21st Woman

Your eyes are too small, go cut them open!
Monolid? What a sight! Your lips don't look
nice.
Your nose is too flat so sharpen it ASAP.
Your face is too round, go cut away your flesh.

Freckles? Ugly. Cover them up!
Blackheads? Yuck. Use a peeling mask.
Wrinkles? Oh gosh! Get a grip!
Your youth is fading. There's no Ctrl + Z.

Your arms are too hairy! Oh, your legs are too!
You don't want to be a monkey now, do you?
Bare face? Come on, layer it up!
Now that's too much, you look like a giraffe.

Hey, hottie! Can I buy you a drink?
WDYM you're not interested?
Why'd you wear that thing?
That skirt is too short if you know what I mean.

Cover up, shut up, act like a lady.
There's no place for you here,
Women sit and polish glassware.

But you better look nice or you're going
nowhere.

"Are you on your period? That's why you're so
mad!"
Emotional creatures, how else can you act?
Wait, are you offended?
Here's some cash for that bag.

Happy birthday! You're turning 30?
Shouldn't you be out with your family on a
Sunday like that?
What? You're not married? And you don't plan
on having kids?
Well, someone's expiring...need another hint?

A woman can't lead, and the glass ceiling is a
hoax!
Makes you feel victimized to overthrow us
folks.
What's a woman good without her man?
Oh, you haven't seen anything yet.

A Kitchen Witch

When I'm in the kitchen,
I'm an adventurer.
Eager to explore behind fridge doors,
Aching to embark on a trip to the stores.

When I'm in the kitchen,
I'm an artist.
Painting with colors and scents,
My heart grows content.

When I'm in the kitchen,
I'm an architect.
Each ingredient I chop, slice, and dice,
Gets rebuilt and reborn with spice.

When I'm in the kitchen,
I'm a magician.
With my dancing arms,
One after another I charm.

Q&A

Does the sun wonder
Why the moon and stars don't play
With people all day?

To Tomorrow

Hello there, future self!
How have you been all this while?
Is it five, seven or ten years from now
That this letter appeared in the mail?

Did I catch you planning another trip?
One of our short journeys to get a grip?
Did we finally find that job
That allows us to grow and think with our
hearts.

Does the sun embrace you in its light?
Does the moon accompany you to sleep at
night?
Oh, how big is our tea collection, maybe coffee
too?
And did you get shelves for all those books?

Are the trees still dancing with the wind?
Are the stars still shining ever so keenly?
Or has the sea level risen so much
That our land has become out of touch.

To Yesterday

Hello there, little me!
How have you been all this while?
Was it five, seven or tens years from now
That this letter appeared in the mail?

Did I catch you returning from a trip?
One of our escapes to get a grip?
Rest assured there'll be more fun to come
Adventure sticks to us like bubble gum!

Growing up was tough with bills
'Twas like swallowing a bitter pill.
There's no Mary Poppins to sing and dance
And to give a spoonful of sugar, no chance.

But things turned out pretty alright
Most things we figured out were quite right!
Groan and grumble all you want
Then brush off that dust and move on.

Travel

Trips lined up back to back.
Reaching destinations with backpacks.
Authentic treasures to see and smell.
Vivid memories in print I bring back.
Endless muses from the world around.
Lush forests, oceans, mountains, and paths.

Dear Stranger

Dear stranger in the streets,
Pardon me, I don't know your name.
But the melody seeping from your earphones,
Is a lovely tune to me, unknown.

Dear stranger on the bus,
Pardon me, I don't know your name.
But the way you twist and braid your hair,
You sure have a certain flair.

Dear stranger at the café,
Pardon me, I don't know your name.
But your taste in coffee caught my eye,
Or rather my nose, as I walked on by.

Dearest stranger I haven't met,
Pardon me, I don't know your name.
But I'm sure we'll meet one day,
Briefly then part our ways.

Friends

Friends
Many and few
Talking, laughing, perhaps even quibbling
But what fun it is
To have company!

Senses

Smell, touch, hearing, sight
Ways to experience life
And the heart feels right.

Ode to books

Little ol' me had the wildest dreams.
Not of emerald fields and sapphire skies,
Nor of rainbows and lullabies.
Just one book and another in hand,
Behold these towering shelves, my friend!

I used to dream the craziest dreams.
Not of fairies and witches of fantasies,
Nor of spaceships to far-flung galaxies.
Just a wooden table to call my own,
Like a king, in books, I built my throne.

I've always dreamt the vividest dreams.
Not of unicorns, centaurs, and magic beans,
Nor of candied roses and sparkling trees.
Just an oil lamp beside my bed,
So I can adventure by lying on my back.

Now I have this fantastical dream.
Of bubbling cauldrons and tea with cream,
And of talking peregrines and iridescent streams.
To voyage the pages of each ancient scroll,
Rhyming and riddling past every troll.

In the last chapter of every book,
With all the effort that it took,
I'll bid farewell to each sage on look.
With one book and another in hand,
More adventures, I bravely demand.

On Fire

Climate change, you inspire me to write,
About how you torture and destroy.
Invading our senses day and night,
Disappointment, is that what you enjoy?

The Millennium Development Goals were a
preamble,
Succeeded by the SDGs, too much trouble?
Now that our future is nothing but a gamble,
For an exclusive party, powerful but
unagreeable.

Now I must away with a readied heart,
Tired of values many in misplacement.
I bid goodbyes as this earth falls apart,
Oh wait, there is no replacement.

Musings of a politics student

Politics
Messy, confusing
Debating, arguing, struggling
Ever so confrontational
Vexing

The Adulting Menu

Adulting
Wondrous yet treacherous
Trying, failing, trying again
It's all part of the journey!
Grow

Chun

Crisp cold wind blowing
A pensive sakura stroll
Rejoicing the soul.

Xia

Baking in the sand
Waves crash to the sand and sing
A song of the sea.

Qiu

Auburn leaves settle
Cinnamon and ginger spice
Embrace and delight.

Dong

Shivering mornings
Wrapped in wool we walk along
Charming silver streets.

Poetry Writing Challenge

There was a young woman in London,
Who sat at her desk for drei Stunden.
Wondering where to find inspiration
To complete BookLeaf's poetry operation
So she can commemorate her time in London!

www.ingramcontent.com/pod-product-compliance
Lightning Source LLC
LaVergne TN
LVHW050257200726
843509LV00015B/3060